Clinton's

"Little White House Lie"

by

Harvey Carroll, Jr

Copyright © 2016 Harvey Carroll, Jr.

This is my second book; my first was "THE UNELECTED PRESIDENT" my Mini-Autobiography. I intend to publish a series of Books under the trademark "THE UNELECTED PRESIDENT" related to the Panama Invasion "Operation Just Cause", the 1st Gulf War "Desert Storm", United Nations "Humanitarian Intervention" into Libya, Ukraine's "Ukraine-Return to Revolution" and more...

ISBN-13:
978-1523910915

ISBN-10:
1523910917

CONTENTS

INTRODUCTION

This short story about Clinton's "Little White House Lie" should be quite informative. You will also realize that President Clinton was under intense pressure that far exceeded JFK's "Cuban Missile Crises."

Most importantly, I hope that you come out thinking a bit differently about the Clinton and Lewinsky sex scandal. For those of you that are a bit young, you can google it. You will find that the scandal resulted in "Impeachment Hearings" during President Clinton's Administration that nearly kicked him out of office...

Hearings were the result from the "Little White House Lie" I had suggested. According to Wikipedia and other open sources there was not sexual intercourse, but sex acts upon the President. Legal discussions that are best found summarized on Wikipedia...

You will also become aware that I

have dealt with many behind the scenes political policy making ventures.

I once had ambitions to be President. I felt that if one is to sit in the Chair, then he must be able to first sit there through experiences...

I have watched a few campaigns, to include this 2016 election and have had thoughts that most candidates think they know everything.

I don't claim to; however, I can claim that I've forgotten more than many of the candidates in the race combined. I've certainly dealt with much more serious issues...

I will touch on a few of those

experiences that would have qualified me to be President. I will not go into details; however, you will quickly get the idea that I have more than paid my dues in the political arena...

You will have to read my other books to really understand the complexities of various policies over the past three decades that America faced that I got involved in... Policies that saved millions of lives and affected the economic fate of nations...

Richmond man says he helped organize Panama invasion, war

By Chad Carlton
Herald-Leader staff writer

If what Harvey Carroll Jr. says is to be believed, he is the most influential international political figure in Kentucky.

Among his claims:

• Named and planned "Operation Just Cause," the U.S. military strike that deposed Panamanian dictator Manuel Noriega.

"I told my CIA contact, 'Why don't we go in with low-intensity action to bring him in,'" Carroll said.

• Helped organize the coalition support for "Operation Desert Storm," the war against Iraq.

"I wasn't a Schwarzkopf out there in the desert," he said. "But I do think my suggestions did bring about a quick end to the war."

Harvey Carroll Jr.

Age: 27

Residence: Richmond

DEDICATION

This book is dedicated to apologize to Monica Lewinsky and President Clinton for placing them in a more scandalous situation.

It is also dedicated to Hillary Clinton so that she can share with the World that her Diplomacy and perhaps even Presidential level shills are without blemish.

To Chelsea Clinton whom I shared this story with in Lexington, Kentucky many years ago, so that she would better understand her father...

To America to realize that talking tough can create tough situations, situations that special interest is eager to exploit at the American blood at the American taxpayers vast expense...

1

OFFER TO HELP PRESIDENT CLINTON

At one time I considered going to work for President Clinton's political consultant James Carville after President Clinton got elected.

I felt that my experience might be needed in the Clinton administration if Saddam were to get out of the box that the world had put him in. So I called Mr. Carville at 11 PM after getting his number from the operator.

I basically asked him for a job and told him a little about my political experience related to "Panama, Desert Strom and Somalia. He told me that he really didn't specialize in international affairs, but suggested that I call his office in Washington, D.C. and we would talk further or leave messages with his staff.

Ms. Hathaway, James Carville's secretary took all the pertinent information. Hathaway called me back a couple of days later, returning Carville's calls and letting everyone know that he was still out promoting his book.

I talked with one of the staffers and emailed some stuff to them. To be honest I wasn't really concerned about having a job, because I had one, and I really enjoyed real estate land development and sales. I just didn't want a newbie's President screwing up our national security.

So, if I had any comments I would email them to Carville and/or call and leave a message. Yet, I didn't use Carville much. I felt that if it were of real national security interest, I would just contact and/or fax the White House directly.

Just by coincidence Iraq started to mobilize troops towards Kuwait's border and President Clinton sent some 30,000 troops and other military supplies to the Middle East. Hence I felt I had to get involved again.

Especially, after President Clinton allowed the Iraqi troops to force a huge number of Iraqi Kurds into Turkey; thereby, driving a political wedge in the informal coalition with Turkey.

Turkey had valuable air bases that the United States and its allies used during the Gulf War. His inexperience cost great coalition assets then and obvious future policies in the Middle East.

I felt I had to get Clintons attention on Iraq a bit so it didn't get out of hand. So, I started the rumor through my old political channels that Iraq attempted to assonate President Bush.

Or at least I don't think any assignation attempt occurred.

I understand a non related incident happened on the other side of the city far away from the former President.

Wars and rumors of war... Only those that are corrupt or evil would manipulate such an event into an all out conflict... Only crazed leaders that would set aside "Constitutional Democracy," and/or manipulate the public for their own gain would consider conflict over this. A threat I didn't feel would come from President Clinton.

Clintons Middle Eastern Policy was a roller coaster ride. It started out very, very incompetent. Secretary of State Albright, whom had been against the Gulf War, flip-flopped and turned into a bit of a "Warmonger" pushing a return for war with Iraq. (Warmonger meaning hawkish...)

I was a bit shocked at her position and reasoning. In my mind this was not what a Secretary of State is supposed to do; they should be Chief Diplomat and Peace Maker. She seemed to want to go to war with Iraq any time they made the news.

Constitutionally and under UN resolutions the U.S. would have been justified to act and maintain a foreign policy presence in the Middle East; however, that policy had to be consistent and competent. Let me first reflect back on a few blunders in the Clinton Administration's Middle Eastern policy and the reason why I say "competent".

The lack of support for the Kurds in the North allowed Iraqi troops to force a Kurdish mass exodus into Turkey. This caused the U.S. to lose some credibility and allow Iraq to begin destabilizing the old Gulf War Multinational Coalition.

A proper response would have been to carpet bomb the Iraqi troops while en route to avoid the mass exodus. This would have allowed the Kurds to establish a much stronger resistance against/within Iraq. Perhaps this would have even led to a Kurdish Constitution and break away a slice of the Iraqi piazza.

This would require working closely with and gaining support of their Turkish neighbors. In my mind I felt that it would be much easier to break Iraq up along sectarian lines than it would be to keep Iraq together in order to diminish future threats and flare ups from Saddam's control of Iraq.

Saddam was diminished to no more than the Mayor of Baghdad. Yet, he still tried to rule with strong man tactics within Iraq. So, it would have been easy and cost affective to just break Iraq up in the future...

There was a need to establish more Iraqi border control to enforce no fly zones and sanctions. Enforce other UN resolutions. Resolutions like keeping weapons inspectors in Iraq, while offering economic development options for Iraq.

It's clear to me that we lost a lot of focus on priority strategic defense regions. Especially, in the Middle East during the initial stage of the Clinton Administration.

This became obvious after later hearing about dropping "Black Ninga's" referring to Special Forces...

I hope that it was not President Clinton, and not General Garrison whom decided to turn my "Missionary Mission" turned Military Mission in Somalia; hence "Black Hawk Down." That operation was pretty much the dropping of "Black Ninja's" Special Forces into a mess that led to the failed mission...

I wrote a book about my suggestions for the Missionary Mission turned "Black Hawk Down"...

Here is the draft cover...

Perhaps the administration didn't do enough to enlarge its presence in the Middle East or they just didn't have good analyst. Yet, the administration did a variety of engagements in the area. Many hurt more than helped.

I was very concerned about President Clinton's cabinet that might wish to influence him back into the Middle East. I was fairly aware of his Secretary of Defense William Cohen and viewed him a definite Hawk.

Sandy Burger while his interest in selling conflict was more on towing the line as opposed to logic. Then there was the Secretary of State Madelyn Albright that was presenting herself as a hawk as opposed to a Diplomat...

I was very concerned that the Clinton Administration polices in the Middle East, ie. Iraq could quickly and easily get out of hand. I did what I could to offer suggestions and prevent a return to Iraq.

It wasn't easy, because President Clinton had hawks in his administration and they jumped on the go fight band wagon at every opportunity, but I knew it would get out of hand if we returned to the Middle East. It would diminish the coalition, world perception of American and force a major economic turn down in a time that the economy was badly in need of serious constructive economic leadership...

Therefore, I felt that it was imperative to get my experience into the Presidents for this and many other reasons. I also felt that is was imperative for the United States to hopefully continue peaceful relations with Middle Eastern nations and promote continued peace and prosperity talks between Israel and their political/religious adversaries within the Middle East.

In my mind, I knew Saddam and how he thought and I felt that he might *be able to out think President Clinton if he didn't have a lot of insight. After all President Clinton was not on the best of terms with the military because they recognized the lack of Commander and Chief experience and the lack of understanding on international security policy.*

However, I wasn't sure that that would cloud President Clinton's decision-making process. So, I really focused on President Clintons strong points of "I feel your pain" understanding and felt that it was imperative to maintain the presence of peace and prosperity in the Middle East. I really felt that Clinton could put a deal together.

Realizing the Clinton Presidential administration needed some help on developing Middle Eastern Policy, I quickly did a bit of homework, printed it out and sent it to Mr. Carville in Washington, DC along with a few newspaper articles on me when I ran for Congress.

I noticed that about a week later President Clinton visited the Middle East, i.e. Israel, Jordan and shuttled to Syria selling peace, an issue that would prove to be very difficult.

A bit later I also stared sharing information to existing Republican contacts to ensure that everyone was on the same page in dealing with Middle Eastern affairs. Here is a response letter that I received from Senator Mitch McConnell whom I also shared my past Gulf War experience.

I also offered to participate in sound Middle Eastern Policy, Peacemaking and issues that directly affected Iraqi policy...

Yet, letters from McConnell were often Hawkish and contrary to

---

constructive policy... I really felt that he was clueless, and obviously a part of the "Beltway Bandits," and leading the corrupt Commissioned Congress under the premise of Defense "Lobbying"... Legalized corruption...

I saw his interest more in borrowing Military funds from his wife's home country China than constructive policy making... I really think it is a dam shame that McConnell and a Commissioned Congress have allowed the economic national security of America to be placed in such a fragile situation.

With all the indictments in Washington, Senator McConnell should be at the top of historical indictments... Perhaps even indicted for treason for his role in shifting America's economic national security into the hands of China...

MITCH McCONNELL
KENTUCKY

COMMITTEE
AGRICULTURE
APPROPRIATIONS
RULES
ETHICS (VICE CHAIRMAN)

United States Senate
WASHINGTON, DC 20510-1702
(202) 224-2541

March 17, 1994

Mr. Harvey Carroll, Jr.
212 East Maxwell
Lexington, Kentucky 40508

Dear Mr. Carroll:

Thank you for taking the time to contact me regarding possible solutions that may bring about a lasting Middle East peace. I am glad you chose to share your thoughts with me.

I am greatly encouraged by the progress that has been made in efforts to forge peace between the Palestinians and Israelis in recent months. I have been a strong supporter of the peace process, and I believe that it is in everyone's interest to look beyond differences and strive to find common ground.

The process is one of give and take, and it requires participants to take huge risks. Regardless of your views on the U.S. policy debate affecting the region, it will be the courage of Israeli Prime Minister Yitzak Rabin and other regional players that will make progress possible.

Again, thanks for taking the time to write. I look forward to hearing from you again.

Sincerely,

MITCH McCONNELL
UNITED STATES SENATOR

MM/cw

I have often corresponded with Senator McConnell, only to receive form letters that really did nothing...

I was shocked and saddened to hear about the assignation of Israeli Prime Minister Yitzak Rabin. I really felt that he was on track to peace.... He was working quite well with the United States allowing us to take the lead and offer real and lasting solutions to Middle East Peace.

An assignation was a major turning point that I was proud of in regards to the promotion of peace. I thought that the Middle East may return to turmoil after the assignation.

In some ways it did as the more hawkish politicians rose to the inner circles of power; however, I was impressed when I watched the Congressional address of Shimon Peres. His speech to congress gave credit to the U.S. for teaching them how to co-exist and live in peace in the Middle East.

This statement made me feel that I, along with all of those that I have worked so hard with had actually accomplished very constructive policy making for the promotion of peace.

I was impressed many times with the Clintons ability to assist in Middle East Peace...

I had made suggestions to build a wall around Israel and try to create a "Co-Existence Zone" which would keep the two parties separated, while offering an area where they could get together and begin peaceful dialogue.

Just too personally celebrate the speech. I stopped off at Senator McConnell's office in Lexington and had them fax a letter to Washington to the Senator offering to continue to help if I could. Yet, I was never impressed with Senator McConnell.

He was always trying to figure out how to spent American tax payers money as opposed to serve the people of Kentucky and America.

McConnell's horrific rise to the powerful Senate Appropriations Committee favored the big defense spending budgets that put money back into his financial support base...

I've always hated the idea that Congress is nothing more than Commissioned salesmen for lobbyist, which rarely represent the people best interest.

We have seen more than a decade and a half of "Commissioned Congress" debt ceiling increases that have placed America's economic security in jeopardy.

The Commissioned Congress will vote for anything and everything that puts a dime in their pockets...

In my opinion, this would certainly include pushing conflict and poor policy that were contrary to America's best interest...

2
CLINTONS'
"LITTLE WHITE HOUSE LIE"

I would like to begin this chapter by mentioning that I presented a copy of much of this chapter and some support information, copies of faxes, telephone log and such to President Clinton's daughter Chelsea at the University of Kentucky in the spring or summer of 2008 when she was on the campaign trail for her mother's run for President.

I assume they didn't want the old issue to come back to haunt them; however, I thought it appropriate to share this information with the Clinton family first hand. Even if they already had copies presented to key Senators like Schumer, White House Counsel and others during the Congressional Impeachment Hearings.

by Harvey Carroll, Jr.

So, here goes President Clinton and "The Little White House Lie" and a lecture/discussing on "Ethics in Public Administration" and a reflection on the "Constitution of The United States of America." Kicked off by quoting [1]Don Menzel verbatim:

"There is no question that the founding fathers believed that a well functioning democracy would require leaders with impeccable moral and ethical credentials. It was expected that those who occupied public office, whether appointed or elected, would demonstrate the highest degree of integrity and conduct themselves in honorable ways. A true democracy with a government that is open and accessible to popular will and thought could only be

---

[1] Verbatim text:
Annual Editions, Public Administration, 2001-2002 (Duskin, 2001), Article 12, Moral Mutes with Ethical Voices (Don Menzel), pp. 67.

achieved by morally committed men and women."

This pretty much sums the Clinton Administration up. The impeachment of President Clinton was a very dividing time for this country.

Most all of America and the World had heard about the sexual relations scandal and the impeachment hearings and we all would have expected the President of the United States to conduct himself much better. And by all means, you wouldn't want the President to be involved in lying to the America People about an explicit sex scandal with a White House Intern (Monica Lewinsky).

The sex scandal led the House of Representatives to impeach President Clinton and forward the case to the Senate for final impeachment proceedings and to possibly relieve William Jefferson Clinton of the duties and responsibilities as President of the Untied States of America.

The side that you haven't heard is that President Clinton may have taken advice to lie for National Security reasons. In fact, I personally made the suggestion for President Clinton to announce a "Little White House Lie", by not to admitting to a sex scandal. I did this by calling and emailing James Carville (President Clintons top Political Consultant).

This obviously placed me and everyone involved in a future ethical dilemma. Even though, ethics are supposed to be high, especially at the Presidential level, I would like to compare and contrast the ethical decision with this verbatim cite:[2]

---

[2] Verbatim text:
Annual Editions, Public Administration, 2001-2002 (Duskin, 2001), Article 13, Ethics Survey, Take the Ethical Climate Survey, (International City/County Management Association (ICMA)), pp. 68.

"Ethical decision making in government is essential to a community's health, vitality, and democracy. Ethical behavior and decisions maintain citizen trust and ensure effective and efficient use of resources."

I offer to you that there are times when making a bit of an unethical decision can achieve the same goals; yet, I ultimately leaned to remember the old saying "honesty is always the best policy" and I think the President learned the same.

Here is my story and how it led to the impeachment hearings of President Clinton. It all started when I sent an urgent fax to a National Security Meeting at the White House, the State Department and the Central Intelligence Agency to try and help resolve a crises situation in International Relations and U.S. Foreign Policy. It was an attempt to try and regain some old "Desert Storm" allies and overt a war with Iraq.

NOTE: Those faxes will remain confidential; however, I will present other material on or about the same time...

To be blunt and quickly to the point; I felt that President Clinton's Administration was rallying the country to go to war with Iraq. Russia and China were siding with Iraq. <u>President Yeltsen of Russian stated that it could lead to WWIII if the United States went into Iraq.</u>

A situation that in my mind was much more of a threat than the Cuban Missile Crises, because you had a major international player involved. Russia and China were supporting the oil rich nation of Iraq ready to defy United States and U.N. Resolutions Mandates. Russian may have lost face during its economic collapse and lost the Cold war by default, but they were no joke... They were desperate in many ways, and had huge internal problems and nationalism was thirsted for. So, it would be easy for a thirst turn to blood...

I saw Russia and the situation that they were in a very real and direct way. They still had a vast military might in the hemisphere and China with major economic statecraft yielding abilities could affect our policy as well.

Both Russia and China were permanent members on the U.N. Security Council and would obviously be against any action. "If" they did team up with Iraq we would have been looking at a near "Armageddon" type of an event.

Both had vast arsenals of nuclear, air, chemical and man power that could be deployed to the region much faster than America.

Now, under the new Clinton Administration; we found ourselves in a very different world than we had under President George Bush. There had been a loss of my once established strong coalition that brought a quick end and world support of "Desert Storm" the first Gulf War. We no longer had a close and reasonable friend like President Gorbachev of Russia.

Therefore, under such different circumstances I felt that all the community intelligence and complex calculus that I was analyzing didn't put President Clinton in a coalition building environment to justify going to war with Iraq. In fact, it could very well spread into World War III like Russian President Yeltzen had threatened.

I was back in college trying to finish a business degree specializing in real estate and finance and I really didn't want to get involved in the Clinton

Administrations Iraqi policy problems. Yet, I knew I had to. I had too much insight into the dealings with Saddam and the region.

I set out to overt the war with Iraq and it ended up being damage control with the Lewinsky scandal as well and the Impeachment Hearings, because I believed that the Neo-Conservative War Hawks wanted to force Clinton into war or they wanted him out of the White House...

Being a private citizen I wasn't restrained by a chain of command. So, from time to time if I felt that this administration or others was doing silly stuff I would try to vocalize my opinion via media tips.

I did a phone interview on CNN Talkback Live voicing my opposition to the Clinton Administrations moves for a confrontation with Iraq; noting that

President Yeltzen had threatened World War III if we invade Iraq and I mentioned that he was a serious man, after all he did bombard his own Parliament in Russia. To give a bit more of an academic perspective I cite verbatim works from Alexander Elder, From Rubles to Dollars; Making Money on Russia's Exploding Financial Frontier that describes the ruthless climb to power by President Yeltzen.[3]

"The 1991 Coup: In August 1991, while Gorbachev was vacationing at a Black Sea Daucha (summer house), they (old Communist) seized control of the central government. The Putchists, as the plotters came to be called, hoped to swing Gorbachev to their side, but, just in case they could not,

[3] Excerpted from Alexander Elder, From Rubles to Dollars: Making Money on Russia's Exploding Financial Frontier. Reprinted with permission from the New York Institute of Finance for (RUSSIA Opposing viewpoints series printed by Greenhaven Press, Inc.,, San Diego, CA 2001). Pg. 96.

they put him and his family under house arrest. The Putchists had been just as incompetent running a coup as they had been running the country in their earlier days. The first thing they did after announcing their takeover on TV was to have a party and drink themselves into a stupor. They never secured the Moscow TV tower, its City Hall, or most other potential resistance centers. Boris Yeltsin, the firebrand president of the Russian Republic, the largest component of the Soviet Union, fired by Gorbachev from the central government just a year earlier, rapidly emerged as the leader of the democratic resistance."

In 1993 a couple years later the communist attempted another coup. I always felt it was pre-planned and felt that the West gave Yeltsen a bit more empathy than what was really going on.

Yeltsin again saw an opportunity to challenge the Duma (The Russian parliament) with the Mafiaism killer coup-de'-ta type approach. Its communist deputies were blocking his political agenda. Yeltsin questioned the legitimacy of political appointed members from the old regime rather than them being elected. Which ultimately could lead to a deadly crisis?[4]

"Moscow communists rushed to the Duma and attacked the TV center in Ostankino on the outskirts of Moscow. The city saw another night of skirmishes: firefights between rebels and the city police, crowds of democracy

---

[4] Excerpted from Alexander Elder, From Rubles to Dollars: Making Money on Russia's Exploding Financial Frontier. Reprinted with permission from the New York Institute of Finance for (RUSSIA Opposing viewpoints series printed by Greenhaven Press, Inc.,, San Diego, CA 2001). Pg. 98.

supporters rallying to build barricades and protect the Ostankino TV tower

The old communist' planning had been slipshod and inefficient as usual. They counted on the support of the army whose officer corps was heavily communists— but the army remained in its barracks. Yeltsin ordered a tank unit from the elite Kantemirov Guards division into the city. The tanks circled the Duma building in the center of Moscow, gave its defenders an ultimatum, and opened fire".

I truly felt that I understood the Middle East and Iraq Policy probably better than anyone else in the world. I also felt that I had a very clear understanding of both Western and Eastern European Policy, i.e. the Russian shifts and quest for real face saving nationalism.

I had to get involved... I would send direct faxes to the White House, the C.I.A., and/or State Department because my old contacts were out of the loop.

The covert fax system was established to prevent the Clinton Administration from going to war with Iraq. I wrote a number of position papers credentializing myself.

I shared verifiable contacts, citing and verifying my policy experience with the Gulf War, and dealing with Middle Eastern and Eastern European Policy. In my faxes to the President, State Department and CIA, I explained as briefly and as clearly that I felt there was no justification to invade Iraq.

I felt that we had Saddam Hussein diminished in power to no more than the

Mayor of Baghdad. I also felt that we had the WMD's or weapons of mass destruction in Iraq under control and/or destroyed them per Iraqi surrender mandates verified by United Nations weapons inspectors and the IAEA.

For years the United Nations had weapons inspectors closely monitored Saddam's weapons programs. The program was designed to destroy weapons that were a threat. This was part of the post 1st Gulf War agreements.

My experience and insight led me to making a call and open discussions with the United States Department of State; however, they were not willing to take notes on the phone the State Department enticed me to write a four page position paper.

NOTE: This paper will not be presented in this book.

They were so insistent that they sent the campus police to pull me out of one of my business classes at Eastern Kentucky University.

I missed classes, and had already taken the initiative to go to the Secret Service Office in Lexington, Ky. so they could fax it to Washington for me because the fax that I had borrowed from my brother Jerry was not working properly.

I did what I could to maintain a paper trail, and have at least one copy of a stamped and faxed a position paper from the Lexington Secret Service Office. Perhaps that fax averted the Clinton Administration from going to war with Iraq.

Here is the paper sent to the State Department via the Lexington, Kentucky based Secret Service Office. This is only Page 1 with Secret Service stamp in the right hand corner... The booklet sent to the White House Council and Impeachment hearings include it and many other classified pages...

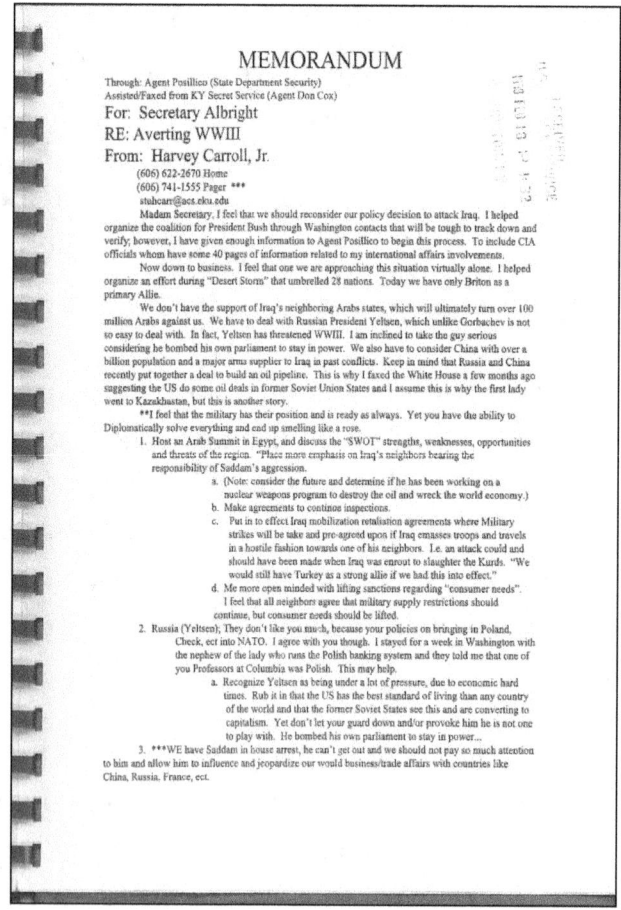

At the time it was a real pain in the ass for me. I had to deal with an international crises issue. Too add to the stress I had returned to University. Seriously, the stress was tough; I was heavily involved in exams, term papers and so forth.

The College Stress Compounded by International Affairs and US Foreign Policy were a bit more than I wanted to endure. Thank God for good medical care, stress management counselors and hot college girls to get my mind off the overwhelming stress.

I'm not condoning President Clinton, but I can see how a few minutes with a lady or "Executive Privilege" can relieve the stress. I can seriously understand the reason the President had ended up trying to release stress through sexual pleasures...

The White House and the intelligence agencies involved were willing to listen so I did what I could as quickly and efficiently as I could. They were willing to listen because; I had a sound track record of providing advice on previous Presidential level issues such as (Panama, Somalia, the beginning stages of Bosnian entrance and exit strategy, and the conflict and peace proposals in the Middle East.

I had helped organize and maintain the multinational coalition against Iraq during "Desert Storm" which saved millions of lives and affected the economic fate of nations. Not bad credentials for a young country boy from Kentucky.

The fax noted keys to rebuilding a coalition for President Clinton and the importance to try and get Russia and other former Soviet Union States to look to the west for a better economic future.

by Harvey Carroll, Jr.

The concept was to offset an oil pipeline deals between Russia and China who where aligning themselves with Iraq, because Iraq was reported as owing Russia 7 billion dollars. Therefore, I sent a fax making the suggestion to do a deal with Kazakhstan and run an oil pipeline back to the west. I felt that this would perhaps offset the China/Russia pipeline deal.

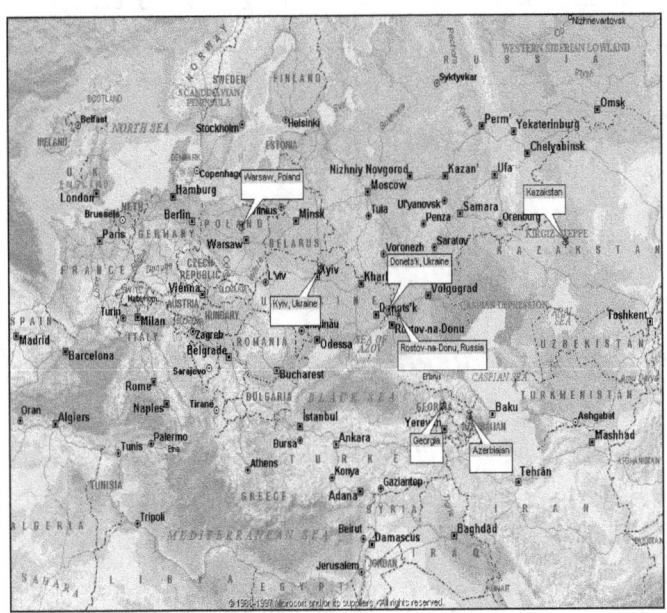

Reflecting back to the day in which I faxed and called the White House. I remember my old girlfriend ████████ asking me what I was doing. I said, I'm watching CNN reporting that there is a National Security meeting being held at the White House...

I said I just faxed the White House about off setting a Russia, China Oil deal in Kazakhstan that will help the situation and possibly overt war in Iraq. So, I'm now calling the White House to have them hand carry the fax to the meeting...

I motioned for her to sit close beside me where she could hear the operated say "Hello White House"; ████████ walked away stating, "Being with you is like living in the Twilight Zone." My girlfriend also stated that if she sees something pertaining to Kazakhstan in the next few days that she might believe what I was telling her to be the truth.

To my girlfriend and to my own surprise the First Lady Hillary Clinton made a sudden announcement that she would be conducting a Diplomatic Mission and immediately flew to Kazakhstan.

NOTE: Phone record will remain classified, but has been presented for verification to the proper authorities, Impeachment Hearing, and Clinton family.

As I mentioned the policy of offsetting the Russia, China Oil pipe line and better dealing to get Russia to put pressure on Iraq in favor of the U.S. was going to take some time and credibility. This is why the First Ladies visit to Eastern Europe was so vital.

While there the press started discussing the Jones incident and then the Lewinsky scandal hit the national and international news.

First Lady Clinton while in Kazakhstan on a Diplomatic Mission trying to protect this country's National Security interest was put in a very serious situation that jeopardized her credibility. Something had to be done and it had to be done quickly.

So, first and foremost, I felt that if the President admitting to any sexual relations it would hurt the credibility of the First Lady. Therefore, I felt that the President should tell a <u>"Little White House Lie"</u> or not admit to any sexual relationship for National Security reasons; and I set out to ensure that the First Lady's' credibility wasn't going to be compromised.

Yes, I know some of you may think that is a cop out; however, if you take the time to give it more considerable analysis. Then and probably only then, would you come to realize the fact that the end justified the means.

The public might also begin to heal and actually understand that the First Lady really was in a very delicate Diplomatic dilemma. A dilemma that required 100% confidence and support from the White House; especially from her husband The President of the United States of America.

In this particular situation it would not only be in the Presidents best interest to back up his wife (The First Lady) on such an important Diplomatic mission, but the United States of American, NATO and other Countries best interest that looked to the United States for leadership.

There was a lot on the First Ladies Shoulders and the President's ability to dodge the big questions. In my opinion, by not admitting to the scandal the President passed on a huge degree of credibility to the First Lady.

Yet, there are those that disagree with me, such as the Harvard Management Communications Letter (President and Fellows of Harvard College.) note:

> [5]**"Don't Deceive**-*There is no right time and place for lying to the media. And while you have no obligation to volunteer damaging or embarrassing information, to deliberately mislead or deceive a journalist is as unwise as it is wrong. "If you're caught, your credibility is shot," Temin says. "That's too high a price to pay. You can spin. You can omit. But never lie."*

I felt that James Carville and the White House could spin the scandal in a constructive way while not hurting the

---

[5] Verbatim text:
Annual Editions, <u>Public Administration</u>, 2001-2002 (Duskin, 2001), Article 9, <u>Handling the Difficult Interview.</u>, (President and Fellows of Harvard College.), pp.57.

Diplomatic mission the First Lady was conducting on behalf of this country. The President could continue to be evasive and not admit to the scandal, while protecting America key national security interest...

To substantiate my line of thinking I would like to offer verbatim writings by Gerald E. Caiden:

[6]*"Chauvinistic and xenophobic regimes placed national interest over all else. Even democratic regimes pull aside the niceties of democracy to put winning the war or winning the peace over all else; the ends justified the means, including the most horrific."*

Granted we were very lucky that this situation wasn't horrific; however, it could have easily gotten out of hand

---

[6] Verbatim text:
Annual Editions, <u>Public Administration</u>, 2001-2002 (Duskin, 2001), Article 11, <u>Public Service Ethics Reform</u> (Gerald E. Caiden), pp. 63.

which would have affected billions of lives. .

The public got sick of the Lewinsky scandal and Clinton lying, so I will not drag this story out. I now take full responsibility for the suggestion that President Clinton tell a "Little White House Lie" to the America people.

I plead that he did it for national security reasons. I provided a Personal Deposition to the Impeachment Panel members, the White House Council etc..

I truly think that my "Personal Deposition" freed Clinton from the "Little White House Lie" and gained vast support from members such as Senator Specter of the Senate Intelligence Committee that voted in Clintons favor...

Note: This may not have been a "Right Wing Conspiracy" like Hillary Clinton stated later, but I think it was a clear push by Neo-Conservative Hawk profiteers to return to a conflict in the Gulf

Page 1 the others are classified:

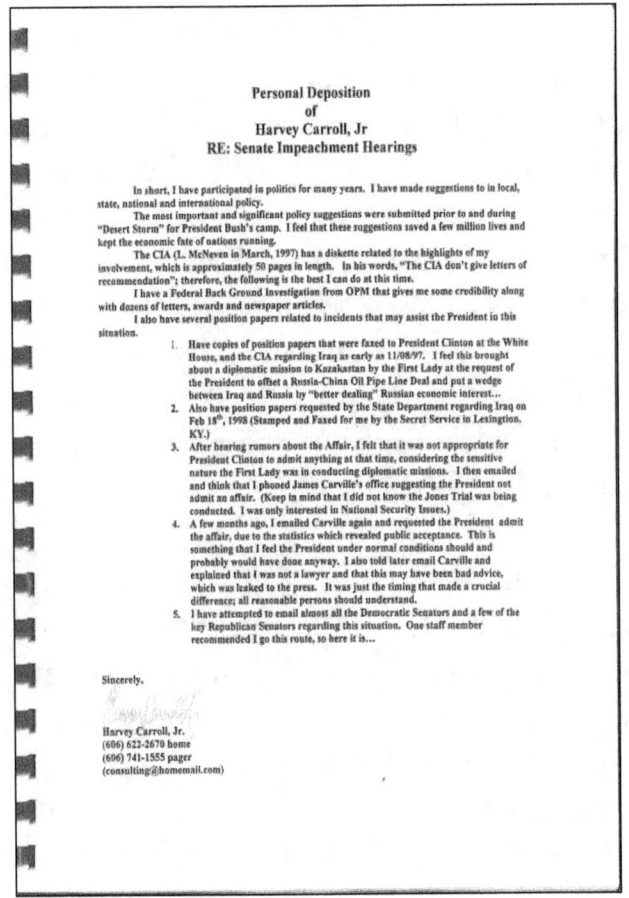

Personal Deposition
of
Harvey Carroll, Jr
RE: Senate Impeachment Hearings

In short, I have participated in politics for many years. I have made suggestions to in local, state, national and international policy.

The most important and significant policy suggestions were submitted prior to and during "Desert Storm" for President Bush's camp. I feel that these suggestions saved a few million lives and kept the economic fate of nations running.

The CIA (L. McNeven in March, 1997) has a diskette related to the highlights of my involvement, which is approximately 50 pages in length. In his words, "The CIA don't give letters of recommendation"; therefore, the following is the best I can do at this time.

I have a Federal Back Ground Investigation from OPM that gives me some credibility along with dozens of letters, awards and newspaper articles.

I also have several position papers related to incidents that may assist the President in this situation.

1. Have copies of position papers that were faxed to President Clinton at the White House, and the CIA regarding Iraq as early as 11/08/97. I feel this brought about a diplomatic mission to Kazakastan by the First Lady at the request of the President to offset a Russia-China Oil Pipe Line Deal and put a wedge between Iraq and Russia by "better dealing" Russian economic interest...

2. Also have position papers requested by the State Department regarding Iraq on Feb 18th, 1998 (Stamped and Faxed for me by the Secret Service in Lexington, KY.)

3. After hearing rumors about the Affair, I felt that it was not appropriate for President Clinton to admit anything at that time, considering the sensitive nature the First Lady was in conducting diplomatic missions. I then emailed and think that I phoned James Carville's office suggesting the President not admit an affair. (Keep in mind that I did not know the Jones Trial was being conducted. I was only interested in National Security Issues.)

4. A few months ago, I emailed Carville again and requested the President admit the affair, due to the statistics which revealed public acceptance. This is something that I feel the President under normal conditions should and probably would have done anyway. I also told later email Carville and explained that I was not a lawyer and that this may have been bad advice, which was leaked to the press. It was just the timing that made a crucial difference; all reasonable persons should understand.

5. I have attempted to email almost all the Democratic Senators and a few of the key Republican Senators regarding this situation. One staff member recommended I go this route, so here it is...

Sincerely,

Harvey Carroll, Jr.
(606) 622-2670 home
(606) 741-1555 pager
(consulting@homemail.com)

3
LEWINSKY
"PAWN SACRAFICE"

Monica Lewinsky was the big looser of the Clinton Administration. She was looking for a Mentor; fell for the needs of a President that had great stress and troubles. Yet, she was not totally innocent; she worked with the Pentagon and was in a Pawn's position to be used... While this did not end up a "Right Wing Conspiracy" it was close to a Defense Conspiracy that was closer to the Hawkish Right Wing policy making, especially, in the Middle East...

There was a huge Chess Game being played. A high stakes game between the United States and Iraq, while Chess Masters were providing side line help from Russia... Yeltzen's threatening of WWIII of Clinton returned to the Middle East landed the First Lady in Eastern Europe on a

Diplomatic Mission, the hawkish Pentagon with Lewinsky as a Pawn was in a compromising situation with President Clinton... All had to be solved; therefore, the "Little White House Lie" took care of the situation with a simple Pawn Sacrifice.

The Pawn Sacrifice allowed for Diplomacy, and unbeknown to me Clintons' prior testimonies allowed the Pentagon and the Right to push for Impeachment. But, the good thing was that a crazy return to Iraq was halted and everyone was playing politics as usual.

The lie prevented the return to war with Iraq. The lie also prevented the U.S./World from not having to see if the Vodka soaked Yeltzen would follow through with his WWIII threats... My guess it would as he bombarded his own Parliament the "Duma" to take power in Russia...

In a weird way Monica Lewinsky became the lady that prevented WWIII...

So, the next time you see Lewinsky don't think of her as giving the President a "BJ", but the lady that was used to prevent the entire World from becoming a Blow Job...

4
VALUE OF DIPLOMACY BUSH BLUNDERS THE RETURN TO IRAQ

I think it is easy to see the benefits from not returning to Iraq. Sadly, I had written Presidential Candidate George W. Bush in attempts to offer advice not to return to Iraq.

Here is the draft book cover...

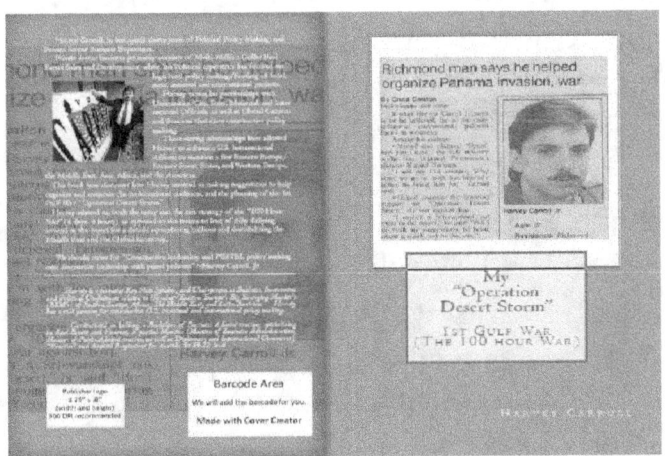

This book goes into details about the development of "Desert Storm" the

1st Gulf War. During Bush, Sr. days, I had worked with U.S. Intelligence to be very affective in moving far beyond special interest in favor of America`s economic and national security.

However, the problem came when I was out maneuvered by special interest as opposed to my voice of reason, but fortunately the 1st Gulf War was quite successful as I outpaced the Special Interest. I had to do the same in their attempts to return to Iraq during the Clinton Administration... It was tough...

Sadly, the return to the Gulf during George W. Bush was the opposite. We know how badly that affected the way the World looks at America as well as the vast problems we have faced in the Global Economy.

I had written Candidate Bush offering to help him as I did his father if

Saddam ever became a problem; however, I never advocated fabricating evidence for a return to Iraq.

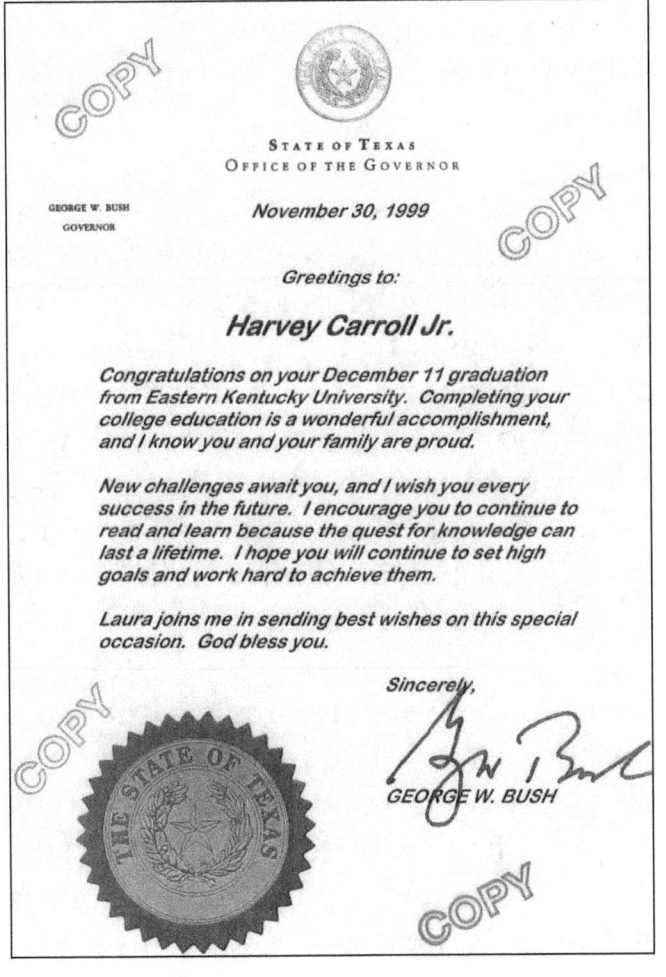

STATE OF TEXAS
OFFICE OF THE GOVERNOR

GEORGE W. BUSH
GOVERNOR

November 30, 1999

Greetings to:

Harvey Carroll Jr.

Congratulations on your December 11 graduation from Eastern Kentucky University. Completing your college education is a wonderful accomplishment, and I know you and your family are proud.

New challenges await you, and I wish you every success in the future. I encourage you to continue to read and learn because the quest for knowledge can last a lifetime. I hope you will continue to set high goals and work hard to achieve them.

Laura joins me in sending best wishes on this special occasion. God bless you.

Sincerely,

GEORGE W. BUSH

I certainly opposed a long term return to Iraq. I knew a long term conflict would destabilize the Middle East and have profound effects on the Global economy. It would also lead to the squandering of trillions of taxpayer dollars.

A Commissioned Congress that was full of Hawks was not looking at reason; they were looking at funding... And they got it at a 2.2 billion a day defense budget that squandered 12 to 18 times more per day than importing of Oil from the Middle East... Bad business, bad diplomacy... The Bush lies didn't help... Clinton's lies saved lives, Bushes cost lives...

I was very impressed that the Clinton Administration stayed the course, stayed on "It's the Economy Stupid" phrase coined by James Carville that led to deficit/debt reduction, a surplus and the greatest economy in the

20'th Century... I had started out helping Bush, Sr., and then became more interested in Ross Perot and felt that much of the concepts were from Perot...

Sadly, my advice and/or abilities did not sell George W. Bush on maintaining the same course... He chose Wars of Choice in both the return to Iraq and Afghanistan.

We know that Ossama bin Laden was hiding in Pakistan. Perhaps someday you might find that I helped find him too after conducting my own investigation into 9/11. Perhaps that will be another book someday...

But, at this point I'm not too eager to write about Terrorism... The World need to get back on track of "Comprehensive Planning" to revitalize the Global economy...

Kidney Cancer and kidney removal slowed me down...

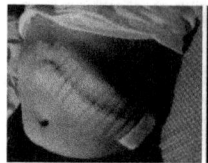 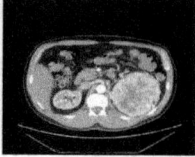 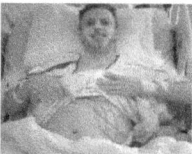

But, I continued to reach out to President Bush voice my concern of his return to Iraq policies.

THE WHITE HOUSE
WASHINGTON

New Year's Day, 2006

The New Year is a time of hope as we reflect on the past and prepare for the future.

The great strength of our Nation lies in the hearts and souls of the American people. This past year, Americans responded with an outpouring of compassion to help the people of the Gulf Coast region recover from one of the most devastating natural disasters in our Nation's history. We remember the victims of the past year's hurricanes and give thanks for the millions of people who opened their hearts, homes, and communities to those in need.

In the past year, we continued our work to spread freedom and peace. In 2005, Iraqis three times exercised their right to vote in free elections, and the Afghan people conducted successful parliamentary elections. In the coming year, America will continue to stand beside these young democracies and lay the foundation of peace for our children and grandchildren.

We appreciate the brave men and women in uniform who protect our country and advance freedom around the world. We are grateful to their families for their support and sacrifice, and we pray for all those who have lost loved ones in freedom's cause. Our Nation will always remember the heroes who have given their lives to protect us all.

As we celebrate the New Year, we give thanks to God for His blessings and ask for His guidance. We look with hope to the year ahead and the many new opportunities the future will bring.

Laura and I send our best wishes for a happy New Year. May God bless you, and may God continue to bless America.

For a very long time I felt responsible for not only Monica Lewinsky being placed in a bad situation.

I also felt bad that I had helped create monsters out of corrupt Defense contractors, which made billions off "no bid contracts" during the 1st Gulf War.

That is just two; I had to deal with the overkill of Panama, the military conversion of the Somalian Missionary Mission... Life was tough these days...

But, my biggest concern was the Defense contractors becoming very powerful and reflecting on President Eisenhower's warnings about an uncontrollable defense department.

As Eisenhower had stated, they were behind the scenes, in a quazi-4th Branch of Government. I felt that they were very involved in the Impeachment of Clinton.

It was even more evident that these corrupt defense contractors later became the Bush base of support. They used their war profits to influence the return to Iraq and to nearly destroyed America in the process.

I'm still shocked that so much money "debt" has been added to the U.S. National Debt since 2000. We went from a bit over 4 trillion to just hitting 19 trillion... It is climbing daily... We must turn America around...

The Clinton's did it in the past; perhaps they can do it again...

5
CONCLUSIONS

The "Little White House Lie" of the Lewinsky Scandal was a glorious God send in so many ways for America. Sadly, the Pawn Sacrifice her so badly, and left a President facing threats of WWIII to lean on her...

The real strong person in the entire situation became First Lady Clinton... She rose to the occasion and delivered with the "Diplomatic Deal" in Eastern Europe... Few people understand the need for a "Russian Reset" better than Hillary Clinton...

Yet, those scandal days have haunted her. It's too bad that she has never discussed just how valuable the scandal became to America...

The "Diplomatic Mission" into Eastern Europe, the meeting with

Yeltzen allowed the scandal to make Lewinsky a stepping stone to her future Secretary of State...

Sad how one kneels and the other steps up on high heels and is elevated to the highest ranks of Government...

Yet, Clinton was a great Secretary of State. Clinton understood the values of "Russian Reset" because having dealt with near WWIII situations during a sex scandal...

This understanding will be very important for the next Presidential Administration. Especially, with Russian President Putin's aggression into Ukraine supporting the DNR and LPR Separatists in Eastern Ukraine as well as the "Blood and Bone Land Bridge" through the territory into the Russian occupied Crimea.

I've spent a great deal of time there and am writing a book "Ukraine Return to Revolution."

I offer to assist any future Presidential Administration with Eastern European i.e. Russia and Ukraine policy development that focuses on Diplomacy, Democracy and Development.

I would also suggest getting the United Nations to present a "Crimean Compromise...

Perhaps a "Duel Federation" that allows both Ukraine and Russia to appoint Governors and a UNDP Representative that focuses on development of Crimea as opposed to death...

(See draft cover.)

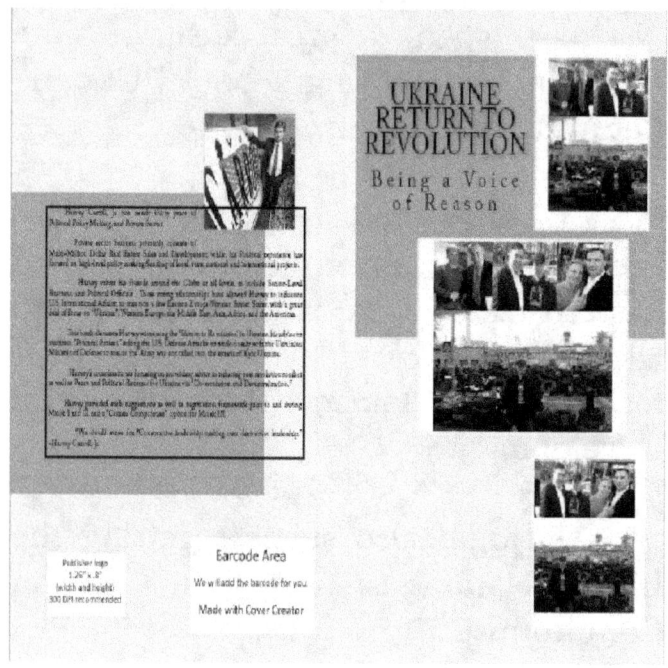

Then there are the secrets to Benghazi, Libya as well... The real events are quite a bit different than the movie "13 Hour the Secret Soldiers of Benghazi."

That film like "Black Hawk Down" took my constructive policy making suggestions of simple "Humanitarian Intervention" and converted into a missionary millions that got people killed...

(Here is another book I'm working on related to Libyan "Humanitarian Intervention.")

Constructive policy making is tough, and takes a lot of thought... Vote wisely...

ABOUT THE AUTHOR
"THE UNELECTED PRESIDENT"

Clinton's — "Little White House Lie."

By

Harvey Carroll, Jr.

I'm a former U.S. Army Military Policeman/Investigator, whom had seen shocking drug related deaths, and investigators bloody shot-out brains laying on their car seats... I now hold a Bachelors of Business Administration Degree specializing in Real Estate and Finance, and three partial Masters in Business, Public Administration as well as Diplomacy and International Commerce...

I've been considered the most influential international political figure in Kentucky-US, and some would say that perhaps in the World at one time. I have dealt with Governors, Senators, Presidents and Foreign Heads of State; and in the process I have saved millions of lives, and affected the economic fate of nations... Yet, I have made mistakes, and even cost lives and often ponder if the "End Justified the Means."

It had always been quite easy for me to deal with complex U.S. National and International Policy. From a young age I dealt with local, state, national and international policy that includes Latin America i.e. "Panama," Middle East (Iraq, Libya, Syria, Israel, Iran), Africa, and even coming to the AID after the collapse of the Soviet Union to protect U.S. and Global Security by suggesting buying out the nuclear weapons to prevent them from ending up on the Black Market for Terrorism, as well as preventing the former fifteen Soviet States against each other.

I also suggested financial bailouts, and another financial AID via the IFC/World Bank for Ukraine that saved seventy-five banks a few years ago (a similar plan presented to the U.S. House and Senate Financial Services Committee "Frank and Dodd" to bailout the American Economy to assist 2/3rds of the American States and Top Banks from Collapse.

More recently, I have shared suggestions to have the OSCE get between the separatist and the Ukrainian Army to the Ukrainian Presidents people tasked to negotiate the Minsk Agreements that may have prevented Ukraine from turning into another Syria...

In the process I have noticed that Russian President Putin sent Troops "Little Green Men" into Crimea much like my suggestions for the "Panama Invasion,." which you're about to read...